THE

BIOGRAPHY

OF A

PAINTING

THE

BiOGRAPHY

OF A

PAiNTiNG

Paragraphic Books

A DIVISION OF GROSSMAN PUBLISHERS
NEW YORK

Library of Congress Catalogue Number: 66-26546

Manufactured in the United States of America by Connecticut Printers.

First Printing

for Bernarda

In 1948, while Henry McBride was still
writing for the New York Sun, I exhibited a painting
to which I had given the somewhat cryptic title
"Allegory". The central image of the painting was one
which I had been developing across a span of months-
a huge Chimera- like beast, its head wreathed
in flames, its body arched across the figures of
four recumbent children. These latter were
dressed in very commonplace clothes, perhaps not
entirely contemporary, but rather as I could draw them and
their details from my own memory.

I had always counted Henry McBride as

a friend and an admirer of my pictures, about which he had written many kind words. Even of this one, he wrote glowingly at first. Then he launched into a strange and angry analysis of the work, attributing to it political motives, suggesting some symbolism of Red Moscow, drawing parallels which I cannot recall accurately, but only in their tone of violence, completing his essay by recommending that I, along with the Red Dean of Canterbury, be deported.

Mr. McBride's review was not the first astonishing piece of analysis of my work that I have read, nor was it the last. Perhaps coming as it did from a critic whom I had looked upon as a friend, it was one of the most disconcerting. In any case, it caused me to undertake a review of my painting "Allegory," to try to assess just for my own enlightenment what really was in the painting, what sort of things go to make up a painting. Of the immediate sources I was fully aware, but I wondered to what extent I could trace the deeper origins, and the less conscious motivations.

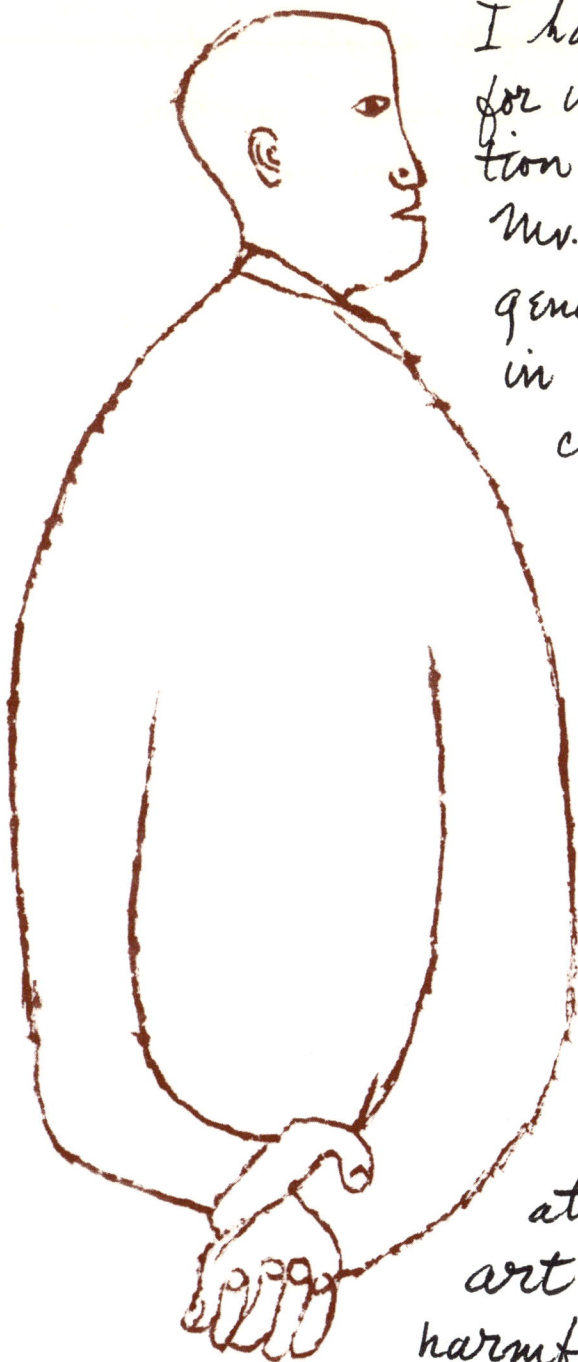

I had an additional reason for undertaking such an exploration besides the picque which Mr. McBride's review had engendered. I had long carried in my mind that famous credo of Clive Bell's, a credo which might well have been erased by time, but which instead has grown to almost tidal proportions and which still constitutes the Procrustean bed into which all art must be either stretched or shrunk. The credo runs as follows: "The representative element in a work of art may or may not be harmful, but it is always irrelevant. For to appreciate a work of art, we must bring with us nothing from life, no knowledge of its affairs and ideas, no familiarity with its emotions."

Once proffered as an isolated opinion, that view of art has now become a very dominant one, is taught in schools, and is laboriously explained in the magazines. Thus, in reconsidering

the elements which I feel have formed the
painting "Allegory," I have had in mind both
critical views, the one which presumed a symbolism beyond or aside from the intention of a
painting, and the other, that which voids the
work of art of any meaning, any emotion
or any intention.

The immediate source of the painting of
the red beast was a Chicago fire in which

a colored man had lost his four children.
John Bartlow Martin had written a concise
reportorial account of the event — one of those
stories which, told in detail, without any
emotionalism being present in the writing itself,
manages to produce a far greater emotional
impact than would a highly colored account.
    I was asked to make drawings for the story
and, after several discussions with the writer,
felt that I had gained enough of the feel of

the situation to proceed. I examined a great deal of factual visual material, and then I discarded all of it. It seemed to me that the implications of this event transcended the immediate story; there was a universality about man's dread of fire, and his suffering from fire. There was a universality in the pity which such a disaster invoked. Even racial injustice, which had played its part in this event, had its overtones. And the relentless poverty which had pursued this man, and which dominated the story, had its own kind of universality.

I now began to devise symbols of an almost abstract nature, to work in terms of such symbols. Then I rejected that approach too. For in the abstracting of an idea one may lose the very intimate humanity, and this deep and common tragedy was above all things human.

I returned to the small family contacts, the familiar experiences of all of us, to the furniture, the clothes, the look of ordinary people, and on that level made my bid for universality and for the compassion that I hoped and believed the narrative would arouse.

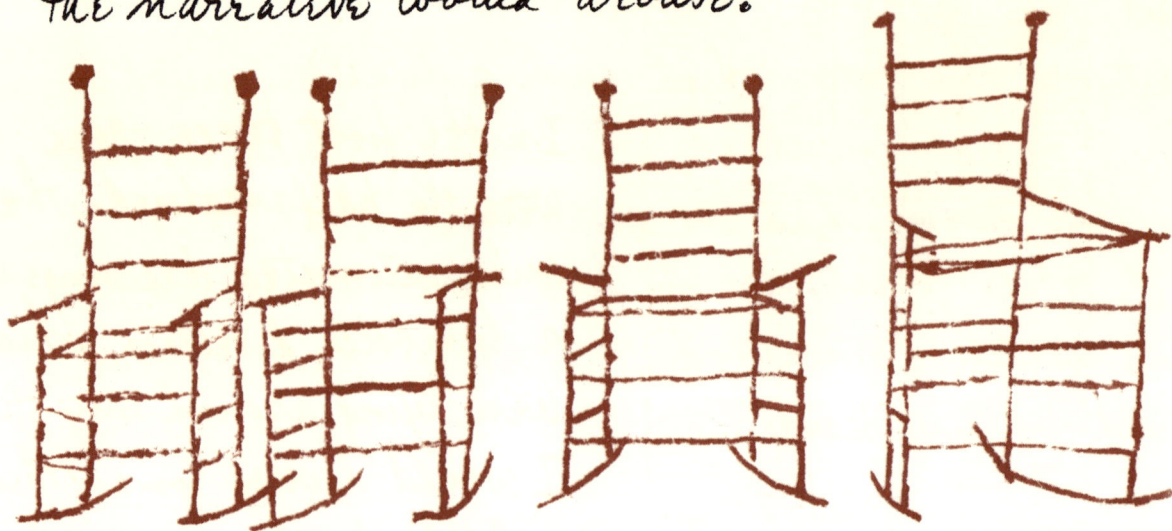

Of all the symbols which I had begun or sought to develop, I retained only one in my illustrations - a highly formalized wreath of flames with which I crowned the plain shape of the house which had burned.

Sometimes, if one is particularly satisfied with a piece of work which he has completed, he may say to himself, "well done" and go on to something else.

Not in this instance, however. I found that I could not dismiss the event about which I had made drawings - the so-called "Hickman Story".

In the first place, there
were the half-realized, the
only intimated drawings in
a symbolic direction which
were lying around my studio;
I would develop some of them
a little further to see what
might become of them.
In the second place there was
the fire itself; I had some
curious sense of responsibility about it, a sort of some
personal involvement. I still had not fully expressed
my sense of the enormity of the Hickman fire;
I had not formulated it in its full proportions;
perhaps it was that I felt that I owed something
more to the victim himself.
One cannot, I think, crowd into drawings a
really towering content of feeling. Drawings may be

small intimate revelations; they may be witty or
biting, they may be fragmentary glimpses of great
feelings or awesome situation, but I feel that
the immense idea asks for a full orchestration
of color, depth, texture, and form.

The narrative of the fire had aroused in me a chain of personal memories. There were two great fires in my own childhood, one only colorful, the other disastrous and unforgettable. Of the first I remember only that the little Russian village in which my grandfather lived burned, and I was there. I remember the excitement, the flames breaking out every where, the lines of men passing buckets to and from the river which ran through the town, the mad woman who had escaped from someone's house during the confusion, and whose face I saw, dead-white in all the reflected color.

The other fire left its mark upon me and all my family, and left its scars on my father's hands and face, for he had clambered up a drain-pipe and taken each of my brothers and sisters and me out of the house one by one, burning himself painfully in the process. Meanwhile our house and all our belongings were consumed and my parents stricken beyond their power to recover.

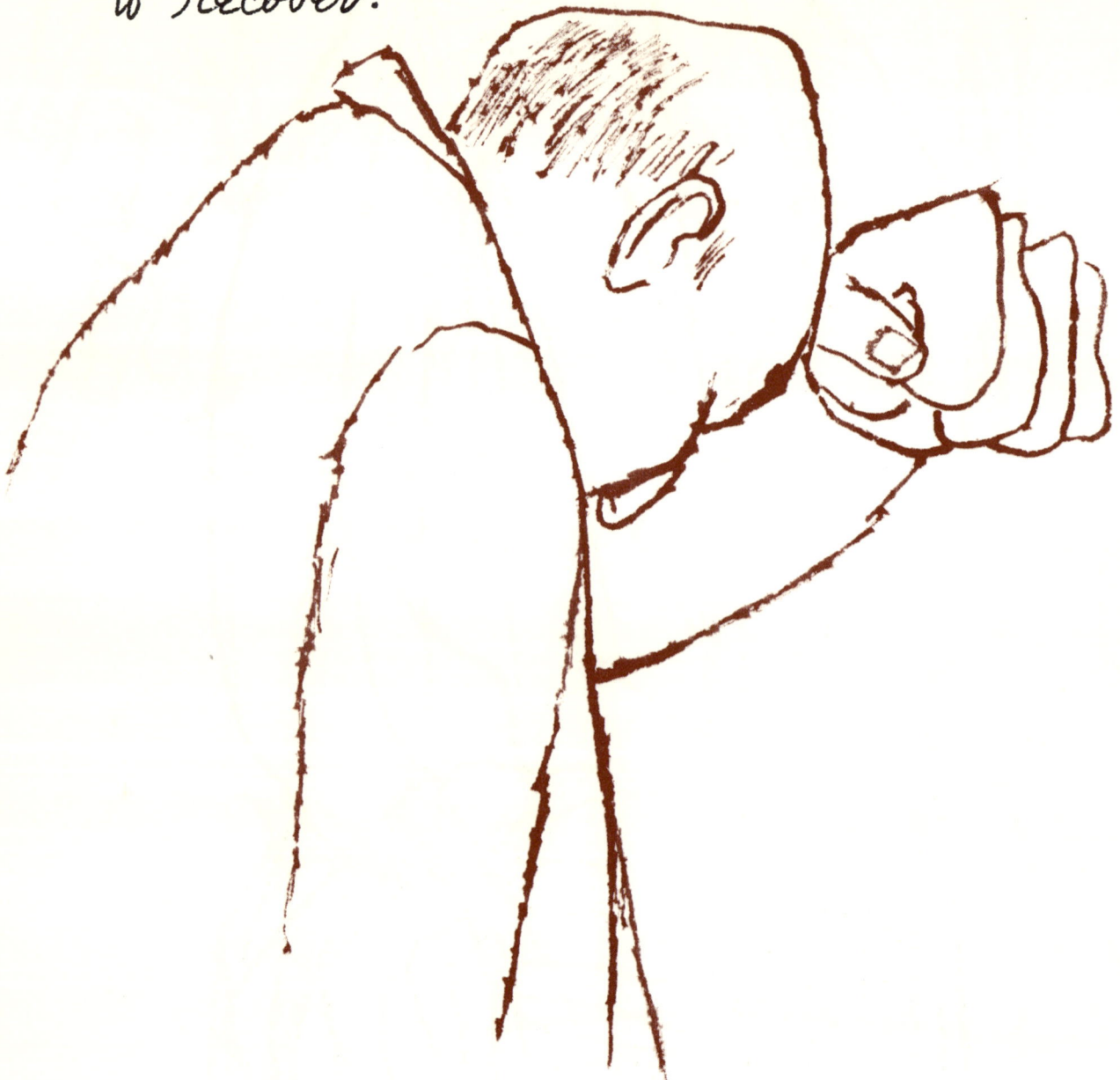

Among my discarded symbols pertaining to the Hickman story, there were a number of heads and bodies of beasts, besides several Harpies, Furies, and other symbolic, semi-classic shapes and figures. Of one of these, a lion-like head, but still not a lion, I made many drawings, each drawing approaching more nearly some inner figure of primitive terror which I was seeking to capture. I was beginning to become familiar with this beast-head. It was you might say, "undercontrol."

Of the other symbols I developed into paintings a good menagerie of Harpies, of birds with human heads, of curious and indecipherable beasts all of which I enjoyed immensely, and each of which held just enough human association for me to be great fun, and held just enough classical allusion to a touch of elegance which I also enjoyed. (And this group of paintings in turn led off into a series of paintings of more or less classical allusion, some only pleasant, but some which like the "City of Dreadful Night" or "Homeric Struggle" were major paintings to me, each having, besides its classical allusion, a great deal of additional motivation.)

When I at last turned the lion-like beast into a painting, I felt able to imbue it with everything that I had ever felt about a fire. I incorporated the highly formalized flames from the Hickman story as a terrible wreath about its head, and under its body I placed the four child figures which, to me, held the sense of all the helpless and the innocent.

The image that I sought to create was not one of disaster; that somehow doesn't interest me. I wanted instead to create the emotional tone the surrounds disaster; you might call it the inner disaster.

In the beast as I worked upon it I recognized a number of creatures; there was something of the stare of an abnormal cat that we once owned that had devoured its own young. And then, there was the wolf.

To me the wolf whether symbolic or real, is perhaps the most paralyzingly dreadful of beasts. Is my fear some instinctive strain out of my Russian background? I don't know. Is it merely the product of some of my mother's colorful tales about being pursued by wolves when she was with a wedding party, or again

when she went alone from her village to another
one nearby? Does it come from reading Gogol?
Whatever its source, my sense of panic concerning
the wolf is real. I sought to implant, or, better,
I recognized something of that sense within
my allegorical beast.

Then to go on with
the wolf-image: I had
I had always found
disconcerting the fam-
iliar sculpture of
Romulus and Remus
being suckled by
the She-Wolf. It had irritated me immensely,

and was a symbol that I abhorred. How I found
that, whether by coincidence or not I am unable
to say, the stance of my imaginary beast was just
that of the great Roman wolf, and that the
children under its belly might almost be
a realization of my vague fears that instead of
suckling the children, the wolf would most
certainly destroy them. But the children, in their
play-clothes of 1908, are not Roman, nor are
they the children of the Hickman fire; they
resemble much more closely my own
brothers and sisters.

Such are a few of the traceable sources of imagery, and of the feeling of a single painting—mine, only because I can know what these sources are, because I am able to follow them backward at least to that point at which they disappear into the limbo of the subconscious, or the unconscious or the instinctive or the merely biological.

But there are many additional components present within a painting, many other factors that modify, impel, restrain and in unison shape the images which finally emerge.

The restraining factors alone wield a powerful, albeit only negative, invisible hand. An artist at work upon a painting must be two people, not one. He must function and act as two people all the time and in several ways. On the one hand, the artist is the imaginer and the producer. But he is also the critic, and here is a critic of such inexorable standards as to have made McBride seem liberal even in his most illiberal moment.

When a painting is merely in the vision-ary stage, the inner critic has already

begun stamping on it. The artist is enthusiastic about some idea that he has. "You cannot," says the critic, "superimpose upon visual material that which is not essentially visual. Your idea is under-developed. You must find an image in which the feeling itself is embedded. An image of a fire? Not at all! A fire is a cheerful affair. It is full of bright colors and moving shapes; it makes everybody happy. It is not your purpose to tell about a fire, not to describe a fire. Not at all; what you want to formulate is the terror, the heart-shaking fear. Now, find the image!"

So the inward critic has stopped the painting before it has even been begun. Then when the artist strips his idea down to emotional images alone and begin slowly, falteringly moving toward some realization, the critic is constantly objecting, constantly chiding, holding the hand back to the image alone, so that the painting remains only that, so that it does not split into two things, one the image, and another the meaning.

I have never met a literary critic of painting who, whatever his sentiments toward the artist, would actually destroy an existing painting

He would regard it as vandalism and would never consider such an act. But the critic within the artist is a ruthless destroyer. He continually rejects the contradictory elements within a painting, the colors that do not act upon other colors and would thus constitute dead places within his work; he rejects insufficient drawing; he rejects forms and colors incompatible with the intention or mood of the piece; he often rejects intention itself and mood itself as banal or derivative. He mightily applauds the good piece of work; he cheers the successful passage; but then if the painting does not come to his standards he casts aside everything and obliterates the whole.

The critic within the artist is prompted by taste, highly personal, experienced, and exacting. He will not tolerate within a painting any element which strays very far from that taste.

During the early French-influenced part of my artistic career, I painted landscapes in a Post-Impressionistic vein, pleasantly peopled with bathers, or I painted nudes, or studies of my friends. The work had a nice professional

look about it, and it rested, I think, on a fairly solid academic training. It was during those years that the inner critic first began to play hari-kari with my insides. With such ironic words as, "It has a nice professional look about it," my inward demon was prone to ridicule or tear down my work in just those terms in which I was wont to admire it.

The questions, "Is that enough? Is that all?" began to plague me. Or, "This may be art, but is it my own art?" And then I began to realize that however professional my work might appear, even however original it might be, it still did not contain the central person which, for good or ill, was myself. The whole stream of events and of thinking and changing thinking, the childhood influences that were still strong in me, my rigorous training as a lithographer with its emphasis upon craft, my several college years with the strong intention to become a biologist, summers at Woods Hole, the probing of the wonders of marine forms, all my views and notions on life and politics, all this material and much more which must constitute the substance of whatever person I was, lay outside

the scope of my own painting. Yes, it was art I was producing, perfectly competent, but it was foreign to me, and the inner critic was rising up against it.

It was under the pressure of such inner rejection that I first began to ask myself what sort of person I really was, and what kind of art could truly coincide with that person. And to bring into this question the matter of taste I felt - or the inner critic felt - that it was both tawdry and trivial to wear the airs and the artistic dress of a society to which I did not belong.

I feel, I even know, that this first step in rejection is a prescence within the fire-image painting of which I had undertaken to speak. The moving toward his inner self is a long pilgrimage for a painter. It offers many temporary successes.

and high points, but there is always the residuum of incomplete realization which impels him onward toward the more adequate image.

Thus there began for me the long artistic tug of war between idea and image.

At first, the danger of such a separation did not appear. For my first disquisition in paint was only semi-serious. My friend Walker Evans and I had decided to set up an exhibition in the barn of a Portuguese family on Cape Cod. He would

exhibit a series of superb photographs which he had
made of the family there; I would exhibit a few
water colors, most of them not yet in exhistence.

At just that time I was absorbed in a
small book which I had picked up in France,
a history of the Dreyfus case. I would do some
exposition of the affair in pictures. So I set to
work and presented the leading malefactors

of the case, the defenders and of course Dreyfus
himself. Under each portrait I lettered in my
best lithographic script a long or short legend
setting forth the role which the original of the
portrait had played in the celebrated affair

LE CAPITAINE DREYFUS

What had been undertaken lightly became very significant in my eyes. Within the Dreyfus pictures I could see a new avenue of expression opening up before me, a means by which I could unfold a great deal of my most personal thinking and feeling without a loss of simplicity. I felt that the very directness of statement of these pictures was a great virtue in itself. And further I felt, and perhaps hoped a little, that such simplicity would prove irritating to the artistic-elite-guard who had already—even at the end of the Twenties, begun to hold forth "disengagement" as the first law of creation.

As artists of a decade or so earlier had delighted to "épater le bourgeois" so I found it pleasant, to borrow a line from Leonard Baskin, to "épater l'avant-garde"

Having returned only recently from France where the Sacco-Vanzetti case was was a national fever, I now turned to that noted drama for the theme of a new group of paintings, and set about revealing the acts and the persons involved with as rigorous a simplicity as I could command.

I was not unmindful of Giotto, and of the simplicity with which he had been able to treat of connected events - each complete in itself, yet all recreating the religious drama, so living a thing to Giotto.

IF IT HAD NOT BEEN FOR THESE THING, I MIGHT HAVE LIVE OUT MY LIFE TALKING AT STREET CORNERS TO SCORNING MEN. I MIGHT HAVE DIE, UNMARKED, UNKNOWN A FAILURE. NOW WE ARE NOT A FAILURE. THIS IS OUR CAREER AND OUR TRIUMPH. NEVER IN OUR FULL LIFE COULD WE HOPE TO DO SUCH WORK FOR TOLERANCE, FOR JOOSTICE, FOR MAN'S ONDERSTANDING OF MAN AS NOW WE DO BY ACCIDENT. OUR WORDS - OUR LIVES - OUR PAINS NOTHING! THE TAKING OF OUR LIVES - LIVES OF A GOOD SHOEMAKER AND A POOR FISH PEDDLER - ALL! THAT LAST MOMENT BELONGS TO US - THAT AGONY IS OUR TRIUMPH.

The ensuing series of pictures was highly reward-
ing to me. I felt that my own work was now
becoming identified with my person. Then there
was the kind of response which met the pictures;
not only did the customary art public receive
the work kindly, but there was also an entirely
new kind of public, a great influx of people
who do not ordinarily visit galleries; journalists
and Italian immigrants and many other
sorts of sympathizers. And then there was the
book about the case which Lincoln Kirstein
sent to me, inscribed, "to Ben Shahn without
whom this crime could never have
been committed."
 I continued to work in terms of pictures
which related to a central theme, the
inner critic being somewhat appeased and
exercising only a certain technical stringency.
A new series of questions now arose for me,
and with them the inevitable consequent
rejections. I began to question the degree of
my belief in the views which I held.
It became uncomfortably apparent to me
that whatever one thinks, as well as whatever
one paints, must be constantly re-examined,

torn apart, if that seems to be indicated, and
reassembled in the light of new attitudes or new
discovery. If one has set for himself the position
that his painting shall not misconstrue his
personal mode of thinking, then he must be
rather unusually alert to just what he does think.

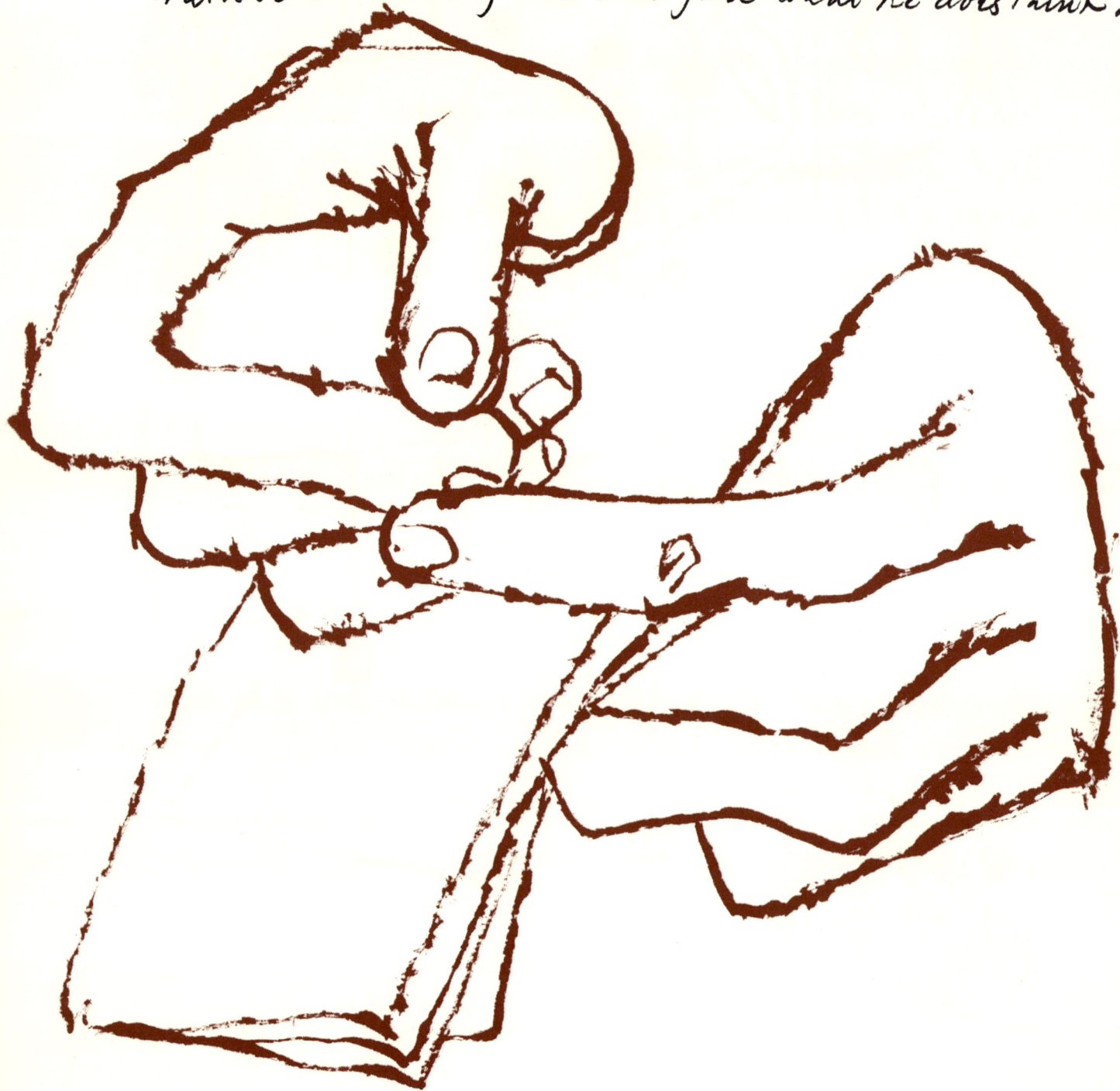

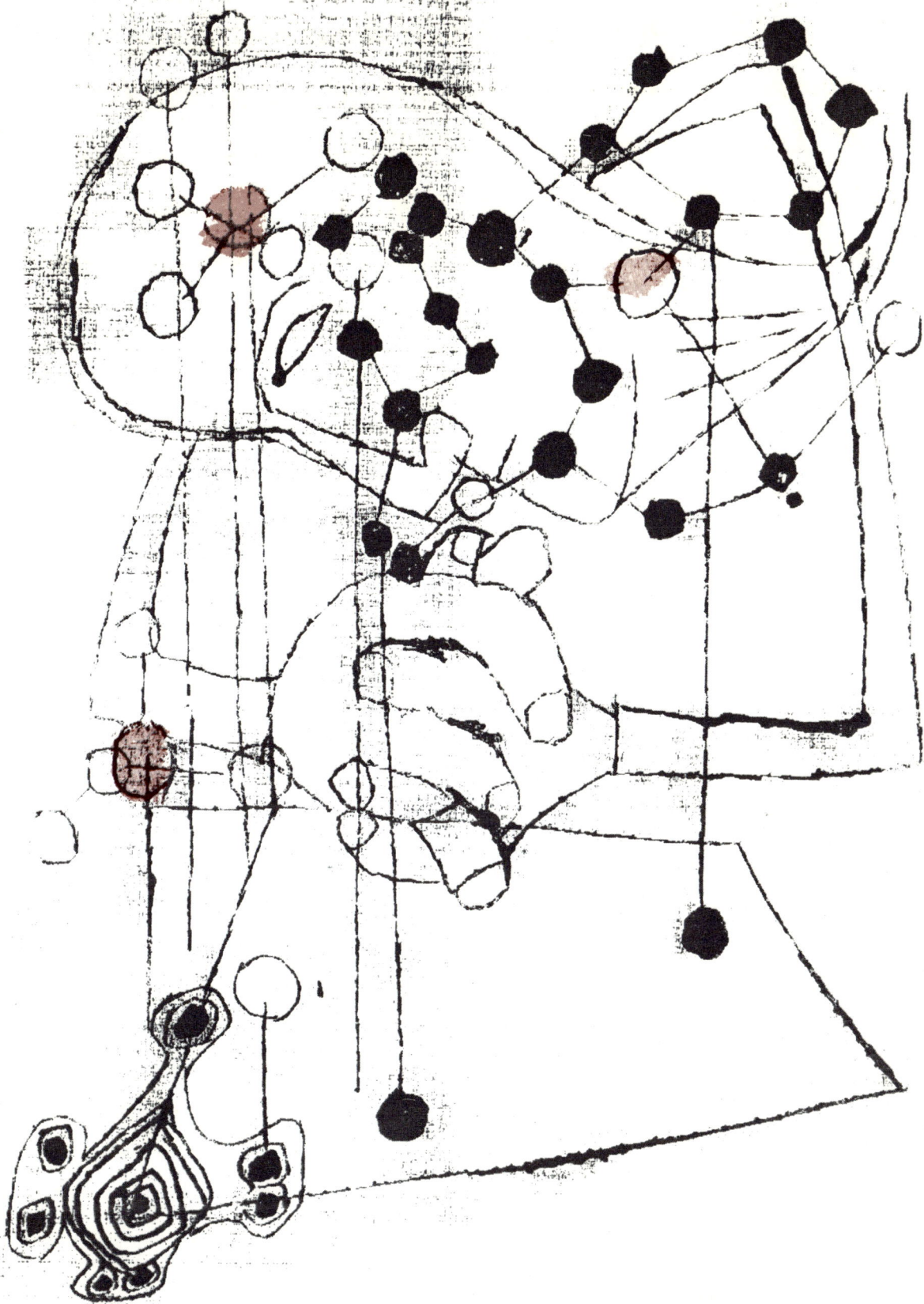

I was impelled to question the social view of man to which I had adhered for a number of years without actually having doubted that it might be either a right view or a natural one to me. Now it dawned upon me that I had always been at war with this idea. Generalities and abstractions and vital statistics had always bored me. Whether in people or in art it was the individual peculiarities that were interesting. One has sympathy with a hurt person, not because he is a generality, but precisely because he is not. Only the individual can imagine, invent or create. The whole audience of art is an audience of individuals. Each of them comes to the painting or sculpture because there he can be told that he, the individual, transcends all classes and flouts all predictions. In the work of art he finds his uniqueness affirmed.

Yes, one rankles at broad injustices, and one ardently hopes for and works toward mass improvements; but that is only because whatever mass there may be is made up of individuals, and each of them is able to feel and have hopes and dreams.

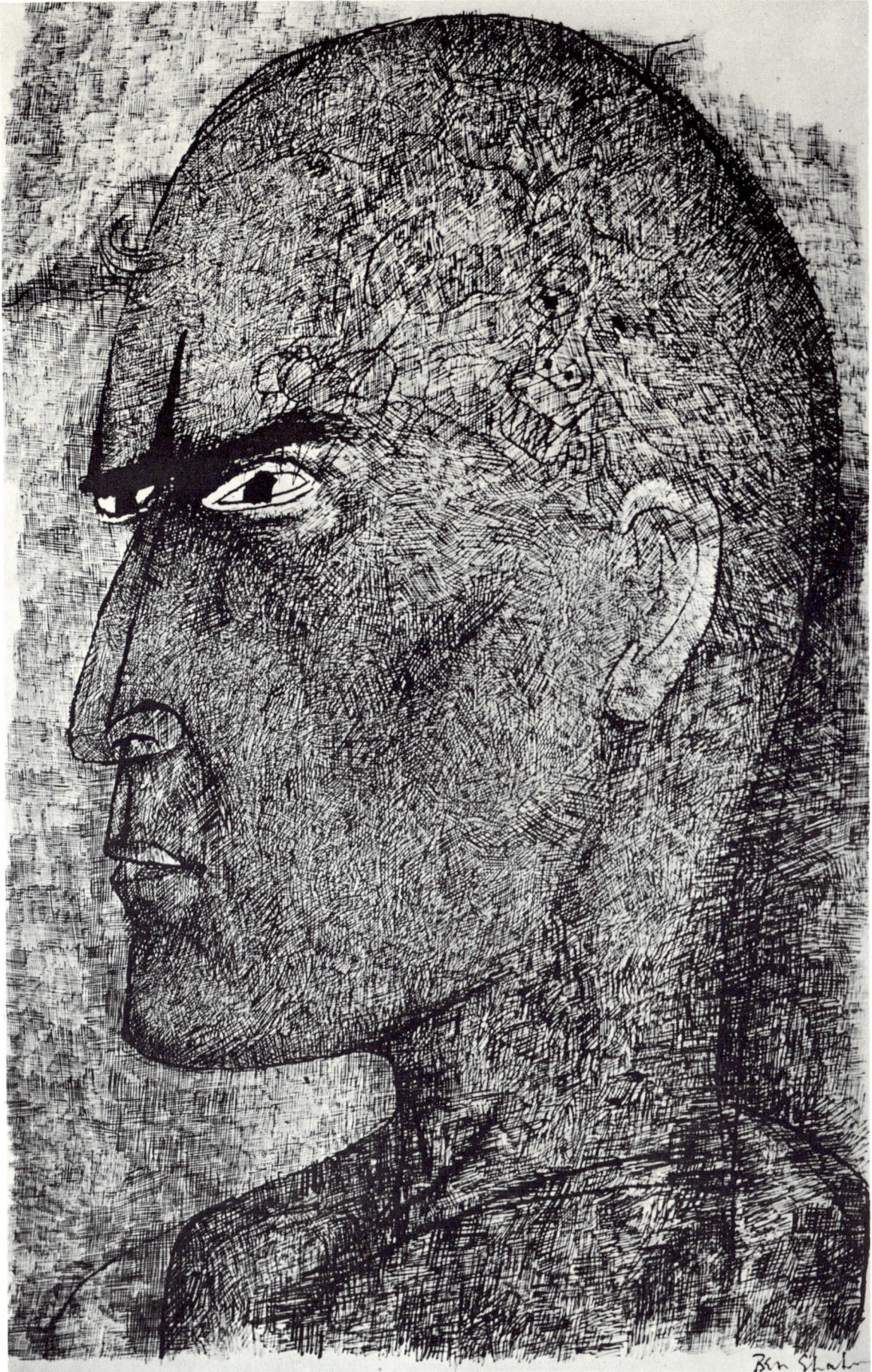

Ben Shahn

Ben Shahn

Nor would such a view invalidate a belief which I had held as to the unifying power of art. I have always believed that the character of a society is largely shaped and determined by its great creative works, that a society is molded upon its epics, and that it imagines in terms of its created things, its cathedrals, its works of art, its musical treasures, its literary and philosophic works. One might say that a public may be so unified because the highly personal experience is held in common by the many individual members of the public. The great moment at which Oedipus in his remorse tears out his eyes is a private moment - one of the deepest inward emotion. And yet that emotion produced by art and many other such private and profound emotions, experiences, images, bound together the Greek people into a great civilization, and bound others all over the earth to them for all time to come.

So I had crossed the terrain of the "social view", and I would not return. At the same time, I feel that all such artistic terrain which one has crossed must to some extent affect or modify his later work. Whatever one

has rejected is in itself a tangible shaping force.
That all such work improves the skill of the
hand or the discernment of the eye is only
a minor consideration. Even of one's thinking,
however much his views may change, one
retains a great deal, rejecting only that which
seems foreign to him or irrelevant.
Or one may wholly reject
the social view of man
and at the same time
cherish its underlying sym-
pathies and its sense
of altruism.

Such a process of acceptance or rejection—
the artist, plus the inner critic—or you
might just say, the informed creator—
is present in the most fragmentary piece
which an artist produces. A small sketch
of Picasso's, a drawing by Rouault, or Manet or
Modigliani, is not to be dismissed as neg-
ligible, for any such piece contains inevitably
the long revolutionary process of taste,
deftness, and personal
view. It is, if brief
still dictated by the
same broad exper-
ience or personal
understanding which
molds the larger
work.

I am not the
only artist who had
been entranced by the
social dream, and
who could no longer
reconcile that view
with the private and
inner objective of art.

As during the Thirties art had been swept by mass ideas, so during the Forties there took place a mass movement toward abstraction. Not only was the social dream rejected, but any dream at all. Many of those names which, during the Thirties, had been affixed to paintings of hypothetical tyrannies and theoretical cures, were now affixed to cubes and cones and drips and swirls of paint. Part

of the work was - and is - beautiful and meaningful; part of it does indeed constitute private experience. A great part of it also represents only the rejection, only the absence of self-commitment.

The change in art, mine included, was accomplished during World War II. For me the change had begun during the late Thirties when I had worked in the Resettlement Administration. I had then crossed and recrossed many sections of the country, and had come to know well

so many people of all kinds of belief and tempera-
ment, which they maintained with a transcendent
indifference to their lot in life. Theories had
melted before such experience. My own painting
then had turned from what is called "social
realism" into a sort of personal realism.
I found the qualities of people a constant pleasure;
there was the coal miner, a cellist, who organ-
ized a quartet for me — the quartet having
three musicians. There was the muralist who

painted the entire end of his barn with scenes
of war and then of plenty, the whole painting entitled
"Uncle Sam Did It All" There were the five
Musgrove brothers who played five harmonicas—
the wonderful names of people, Plato Jordan
and Jasper Lancaster, and of towns, Pity Me, and
Tail Holt, and Bird-in-Hand. There were the poor
who were rich in spirit, and the rich who were
also sometimes rich in spirit. There was the
South and its story-telling art, stories of snakes
and storms and haunted houses, enchanting;
and yet such talent thriving in the same human
shell with with hopeless prejudices, bigotry,
and ignorance.

Personal realism, personal observation
of the way of people, the mood of life and
places; all that is a great pleasure, but I
felt some larger potentiality in art.

During the war I functioned within the
Office of War Information. We were supplied
with a constant stream of material, photographic
and other kinds of documentation of the
decimation within enemy territory. There were
the secret confidential horrible facts of the
cartloads of dead; Greece, India, Poland.

There were the blurred pictures of bombed-out
places, so many of which I knew well and cherished.
There were the churches destroyed, the villages,
the monasteries—Monte Cassino and Ravenna. At
that time I painted only one theme, "Europa," you
might call it. Particularly I painted Italy as I
lamented it, or feared that it might have become.

It had been my principle in painting, during
all the changes which I had undertaken, that
outer objects, or people, must be observed with

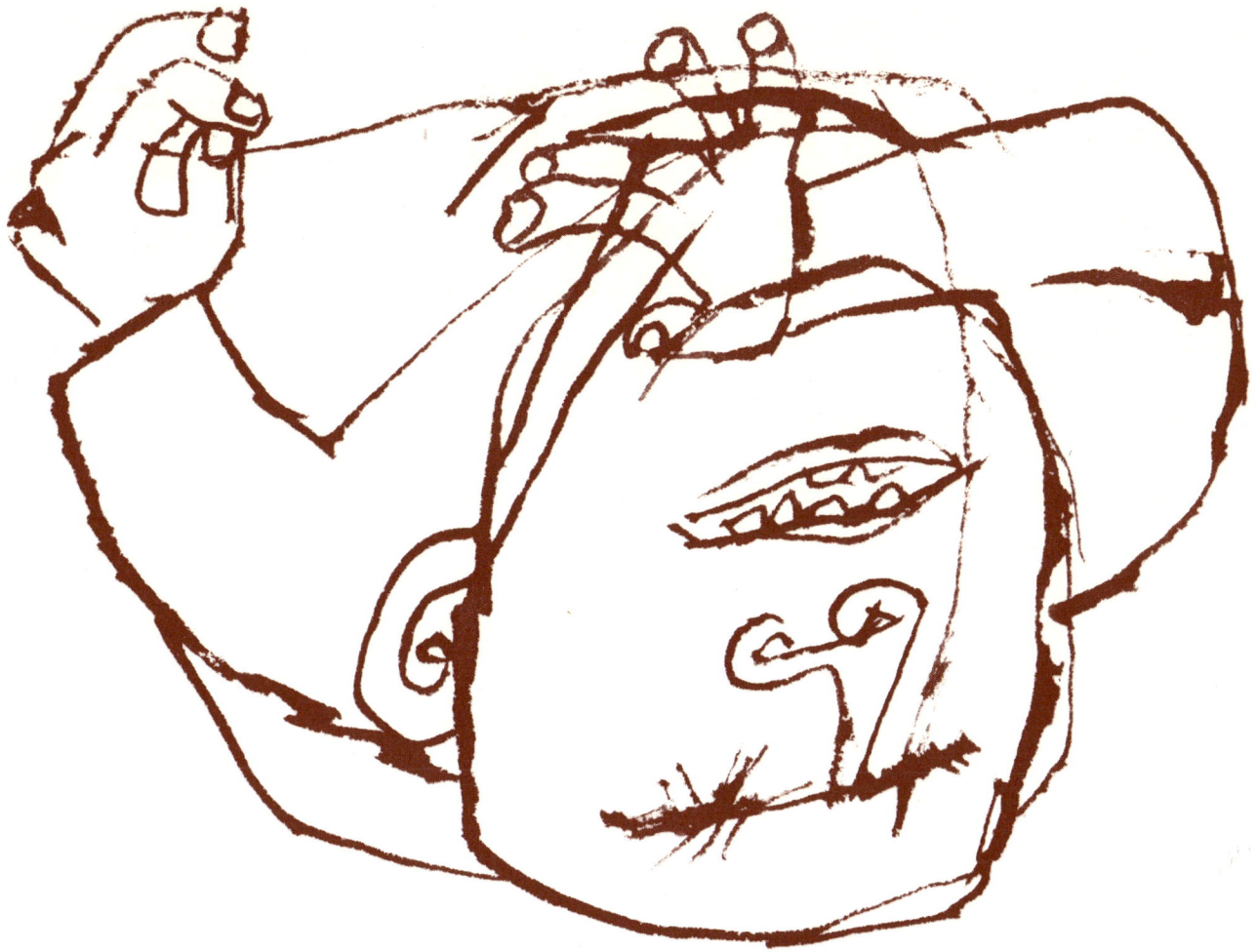

an acute eye for detail, but that all such observ-
ations must be molded from an inner view.
I had felt consistantly, also, that any such
material must be painted in a way wholly
subject to the kind of medium, whether oil,
tempera, fresco, or what ever

But now I saw art turning abstract, courting material alone. It seemed to me that such a direction promised only a cul-de-sac for the painter. I wanted to avoid that direction, and at the same time I wanted to find some deeper source of meaning in art, a constant spring that would not run dry with the next change in political weather.

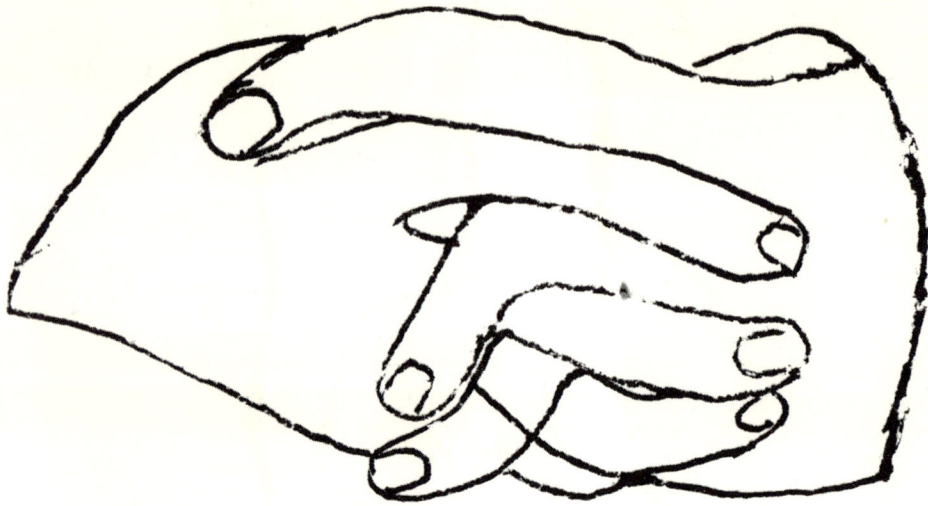

Among the battery of acceptances and rejections that mold the style of a painter, there rises a force not only his own growing and changing work, but that of other work, both contemporary and past. He must observe all such direction and perhaps continue those which appear to be fruitful, while shunning those which appear to be limited and of short duration. Thus a degree of sophistication is essential to the painter.

Ben Shahn

While I felt a growing conviction as to the validity of the inner view, I wanted not to re-tread the ground which had been so admirably illuminated by Surrealism. Indeed the subconscious, the unconscious, the dream-world does offer a rich, an almost limitless, panorama for the explorations of art; but in that approach, I think we may call it the psychological approach, one may discern beyond the rich imagery, certain limits and inevitable pitfalls.

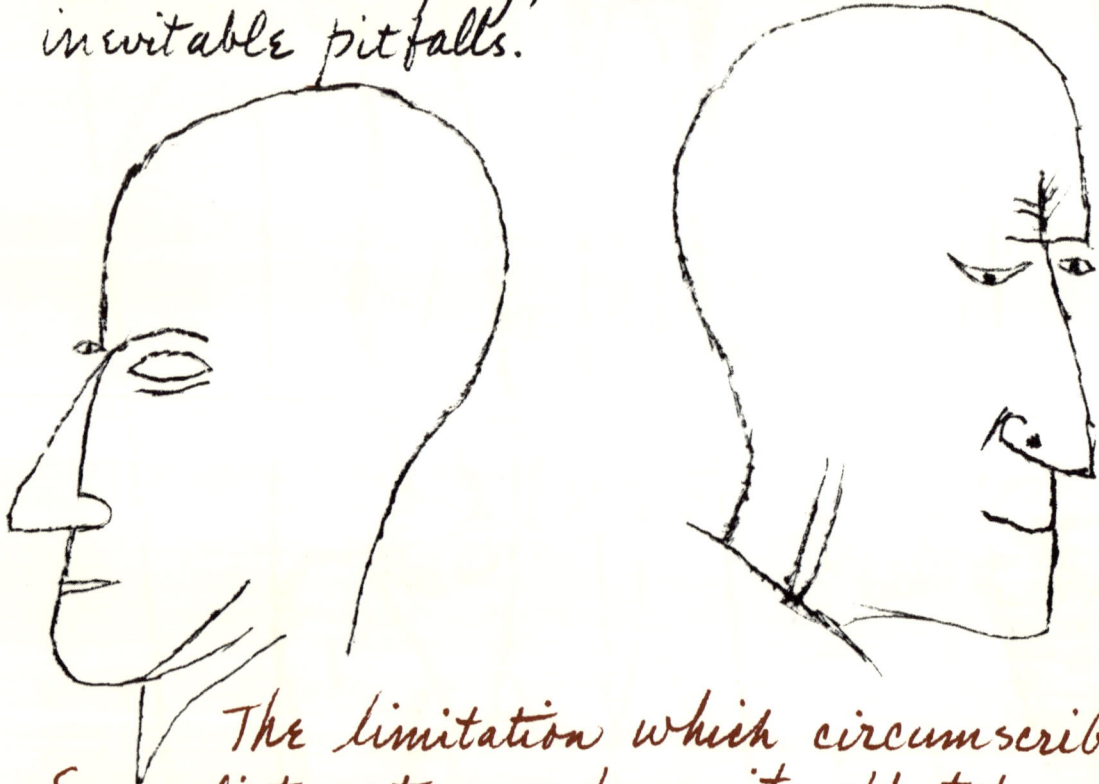

The limitation which circumscribed Surrealist art arose from its effort to reveal the subconscious. For in that effort control and intentions were increasingly relinquished. Surrealism and the psychological approach led into that quagmire of the so called automatic practices practices of art — the biomorphic, the fecal, the fetal, and other absurdities.

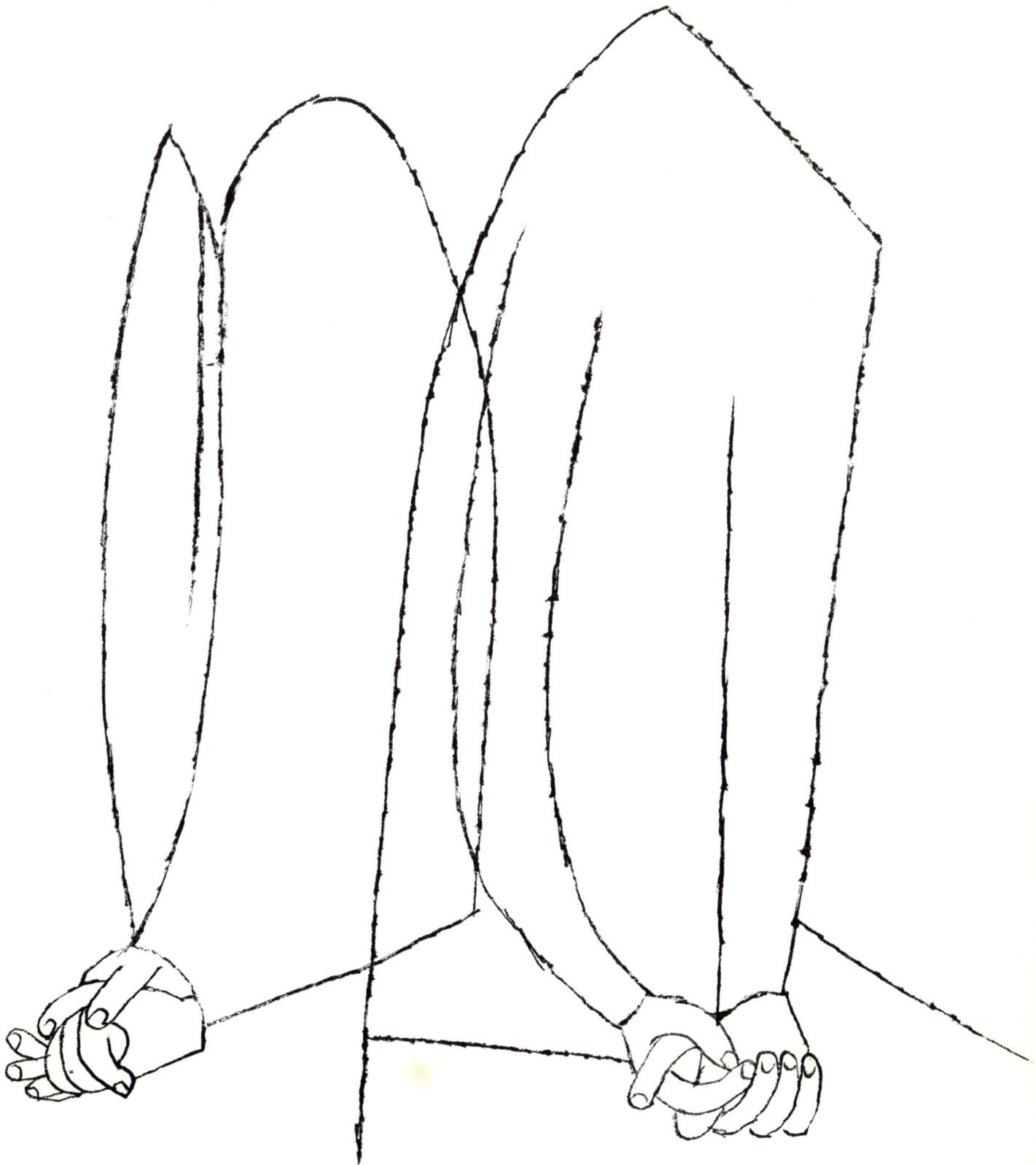

The subconscious may greatly shape one's art; undoubtedly it does so. But the subconscious cannot create art. The very act of making a painting is an intending one; thus to intend and at the same time to relinquish intention is a hopeless contradiction, albeit one that is exhibited on every hand.

But the great failure of all such art, at least in my own view, lies in the fact that man's most able self is his conscious self — his intending self. The psychological view can at best, even assuming it to be accurate, tell us what man is in spite of himself. It may perhaps discover those animal motives which are said to lurk beneath the human ones. It may unmask selfish purposes lying within altruism. It may even be able to reveal primitive psychological states underneath the claims and achievements of philosophy — the brute beneath the intellect. But the value of man, if he has any at all, resides in his intentions, in the degree to which he has moved away from the brute, in his intellect at its peak and in his humanity at its peak.

Ben Shahn

I do not conceive it to be the role of art to retrogress either into the pre-natal or into the pre-human state. So while I accept the vast inner landscape that extends off the boundaries of consciousness to be almost infinitely fruitful of images and symbols, I know that such images mean one thing to the psychologist and quite another to the artist.

One might return to Oedipus. For to the psychologist, Oedipus is a symbol of aberration only — a medical symbol. But to the artist Oedipus is a symbol of moral anguish, and even more than that, of transcendent spiritual power.

Or, consider Van Gogh; to the psychologist it is the periodic insanity of Van Gogh that is pre-eminent, and the psychologist deduces much from that. But to the artist it is clear that it was the great love of things and of people and the incredible suffering of Van Gogh that made his art possible and his insanity inevitable.

I know that there must be an ingredient of complete belief in any work of art—

belief in what one is doing. I do not doubt that those artists who work only for pure form believe in form alone as the ultimate possible expression in art. Those who look upon their art as therapy probably believe with equal fervor in what they are doing. And I am sure that the artists who only manipulate materials believe firmly in that method. But here again one must be impelled by rejection. Such art can contain nothing of experience either inward or outward. It is only a painted curtain resting mid way between the subjective and the objective, closing either off from the other.

To me both subjective and objective are of paramount importance, another aspect of the problem of image and idea. The challenge is not to abolish both from art, but rather to unite them into a single impression, an image of which meaning is an inalienable part.

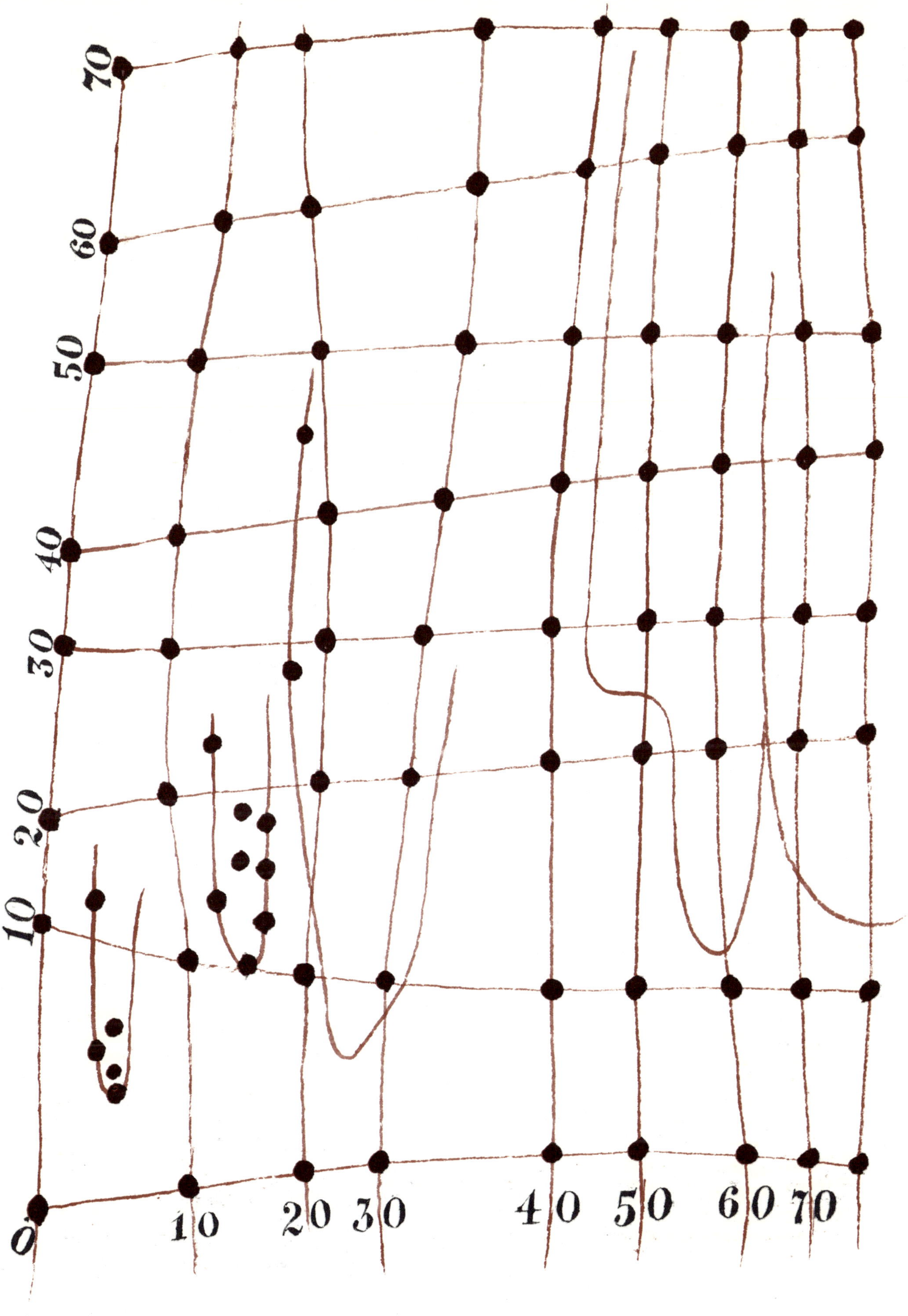
0
10
20
30
40
50
60
70
10
20
30
40
50
60
70

I had once believed that the incidental, the individual, and the topical were enough, that in such instances of life all of life could be implied.

But then I came to feel that that is not enough. I have wanted to reach farther, to tap some sort of universal experience, to create symbols that will have some such universal quality.

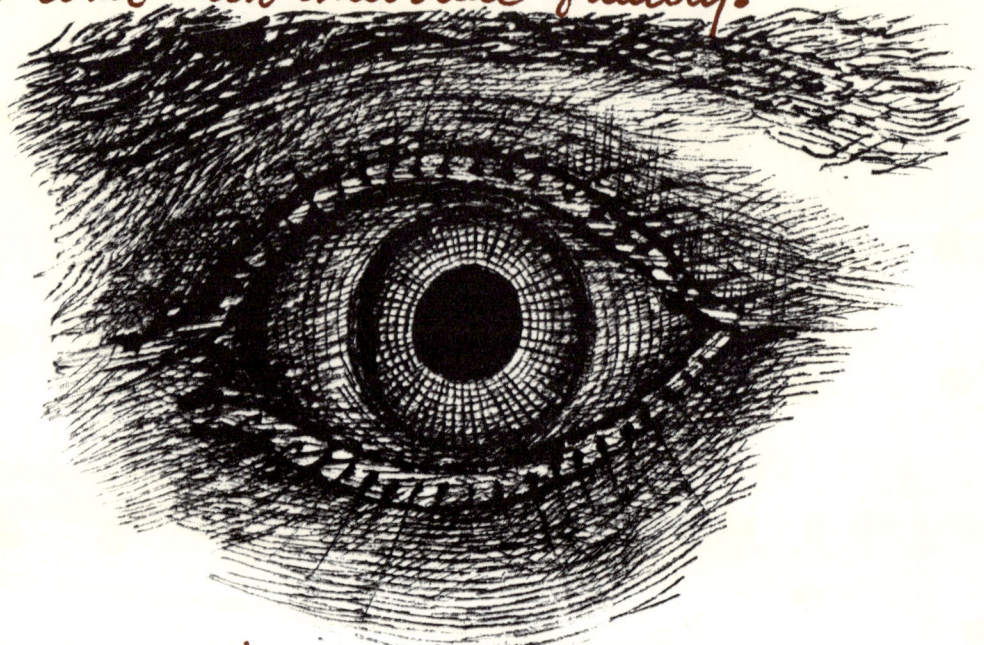

I made a series of paintings during the war which, in my own view - and what other view has an artist? - began to realize this more difficult objective. I shall discuss the pictures themselves, but again it is necessary to emphasize the conflict which arises in any such change of view, and the painful necessity to be aware of what one really thinks and wants in art.

This is Nazi brutality

RADIO BERLIN. -- IT IS OFFICIALLY ANNOUNCED: -
ALL MEN OF LIDICE - CZECHOSLOVAKIA - HAVE BEEN SHOT:
THE WOMEN DEPORTED TO A CONCENTRATION CAMP:
THE CHILDREN SENT TO APPROPRIATE CENTERS-- THE
NAME OF THE VILLAGE WAS IMMEDIATELY ABOLISHED.
6/11/42/115P

I have already mentioned my personal dislike of generalities. Now, one must ask, is not the universal merely another term for the generality? How can one actually achieve a universality in painting without becoming merely more generalized and abstract? I feel that this question is one which greatly concerns artists. Its resolution will greatly affect the kind of an artist one is to be.

My own approach could only be to ask myself just why it is that I so dislike all statistics and most generalities. The answer that I found was simply that I dislike such material because it is impersonal. In being average to all things, it is particular to none. If we were to attempt to construct an "average American" we would necessarily put together an effigy which would have the common qualities, peculiarities, and unique qualities of no American. It would, like the David Reisman statistical high school student, approximate everyone and resemble no one.

But let us say that the universal is that unique thing which affirms the unique qualities of all things. The universal qualities

of all things. The universal experience is that
private experience which illuminates the
private and personal world in which
each of us lives the major part of his life.
Thus, in art, the symbol which has vast
universality may be some figure drawn
from the most remote and inward recesses
of consciousness; for it is here that we are
unique and sovereign and most wholly
aware. I think of Masaccio's "Expulsion
from the Garden," so intensely personal that
it leaves no person untouched. I think
of a Chirico figure, lonely in a lonely street
haunted by shadows, its loneliness speaking
to all human loneliness. As an experience
neither painting has anything of the average;
both come from extreme limits of feeling.
and both paintings have a great universality.

The paintings which I made toward the close
of the war — the "Liberation" picture, "the Red
Staircase" Cherubs and Children", Italian Landscape" and quite a number of others did not
perhaps depart sharply in style or appearance
from my earlier work, but they had become more
private and more inward looking ǂ symbolism which

which I might once have considered cryptic
now became the only means by which I could formulate the sense of emptiness and waste that
the war gave me, and the sense of littleness
of people trying to live on through the enormity
of war. I think that at that time I was very little
concerned with communication as a conscious
objective. Formulation itself was enough of a problem.
To formulate into into images, into painted
surfaces, feelings which, if obscure, were at least
strongly felt.

But in my own view these paintings were successful. I found in them a way to go, actually a liberation of sorts for myself. I became most conscious then that the emotional image is not necessarily of that event in the outside world which prompts our feeling; the emotional image is rather made up of the inner vestiges of many events. It is of that company of phantoms which we all own and which have no other sense than the fear sense, or that of the ludicrous, or of the terribly

beautiful; images that have the nostalgia of
childhood with possibly none of the facts of our
childhood; images which may be drawn only
from the recollection of paint upon a surface,
and yet that have given us great exaltation —
such are the images to be sensed and
formulated.

I became increasingly preoccupied with the

sense of the look, indeed with the power, of this
newly emerging order image. It was as I have
indicated, a product of active intentions plus
the constant demands and rejections of the
inward critic; even perhaps of a certain striving
to measure my own work critically with some
basic truth in art. At the same time I do read
copious remarks about my work by outer critics,
some referring to the work as "social realism",
some lamenting its degree of content which

they hold to be irrelevant to any art, but most employ-
ing certain labels which, however friendly they may
be in intention, have so little relation to the context
of a painting. I believe that if it were left to artists
to choose their own labels most would choose none.
For most artists have expended a great deal
of energy in scrambling out of classes and
categories and pigeon-holes, aspiring toward
some state of perfect freedom which un-
fortunately neither human limitations
nor the law allows - not to mention
the critic.

Ben Shahn

I just don't think, I know that this long historical process which I have just described is present within the one painting of the fire animal which is called "Allegory." There is considerable content which extends through one's work, appearing, disappearing, changing, growing; there is the shaping power of rejection which I have discussed, and the constant activity of revising one's ideas — of thinking what one wants to think. All these elements are present to a greater or less degree in the work of any painter who is deeply occupied in trying to impress his personality upon inert matter

But allowing all this procedure and material, I must now say that it is in another sense only background. It is formulative of taste; it is the stuff and make-up of the inner critic; it is the underground stream of ideas. But idea itself must always bow to the needs and demands of the material in which it is to be cast. The painter who stands before an empty canvas must think in terms of paint. If he is just beginning in the use of paint, the way may be extremely

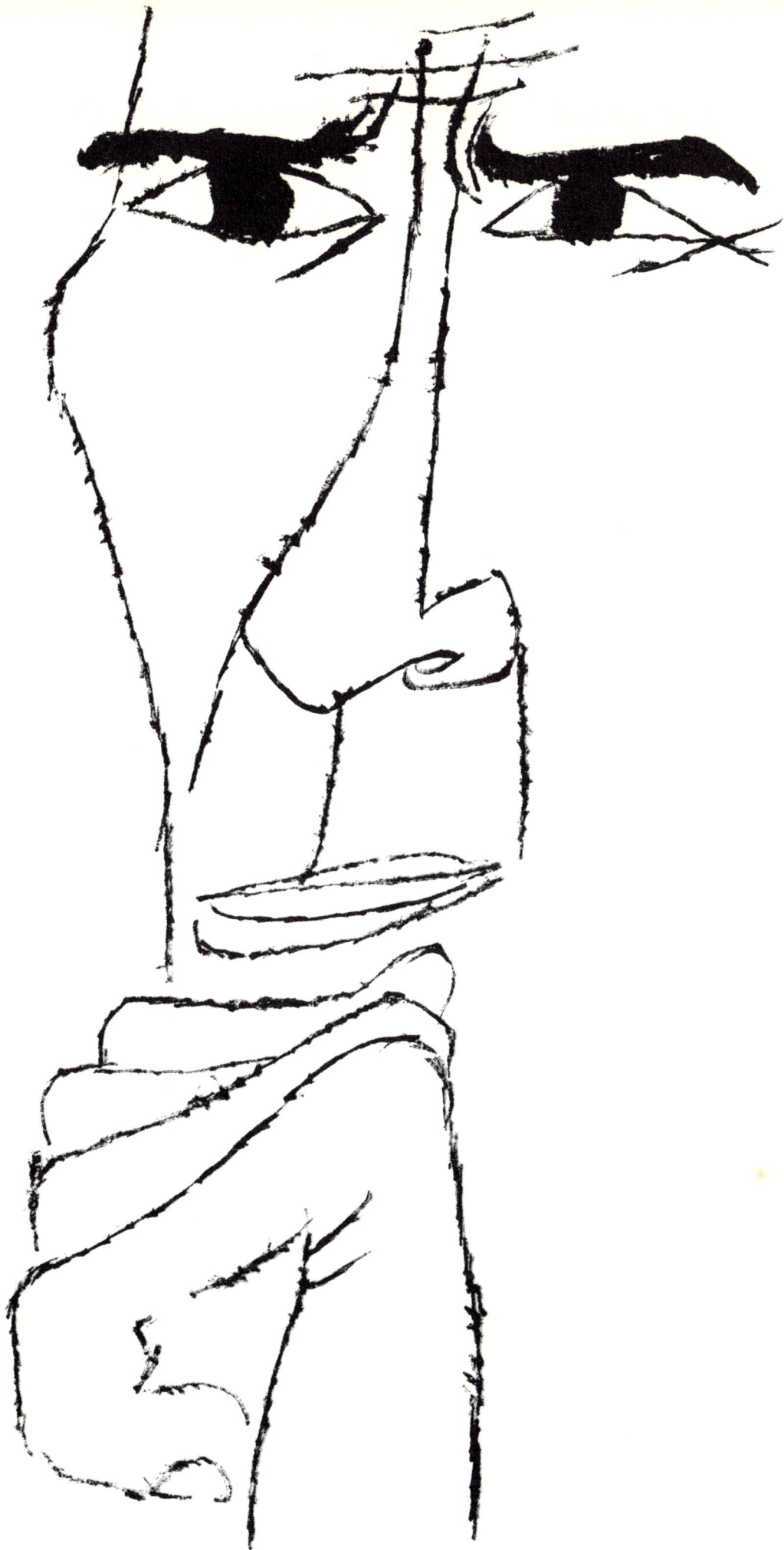

difficult for him because he may not yet have established a complete rapport with his medium. He does not yet know what it can do, and what it cannot do. He has not yet discovered that paint has a power by itself and in itself - or where the power lies, or how it relates to him. For with the practiced it is that relationship which counts; his inner images are paint images, as those of the poet are no doubt metrical word images and those of the musicians tonal images.

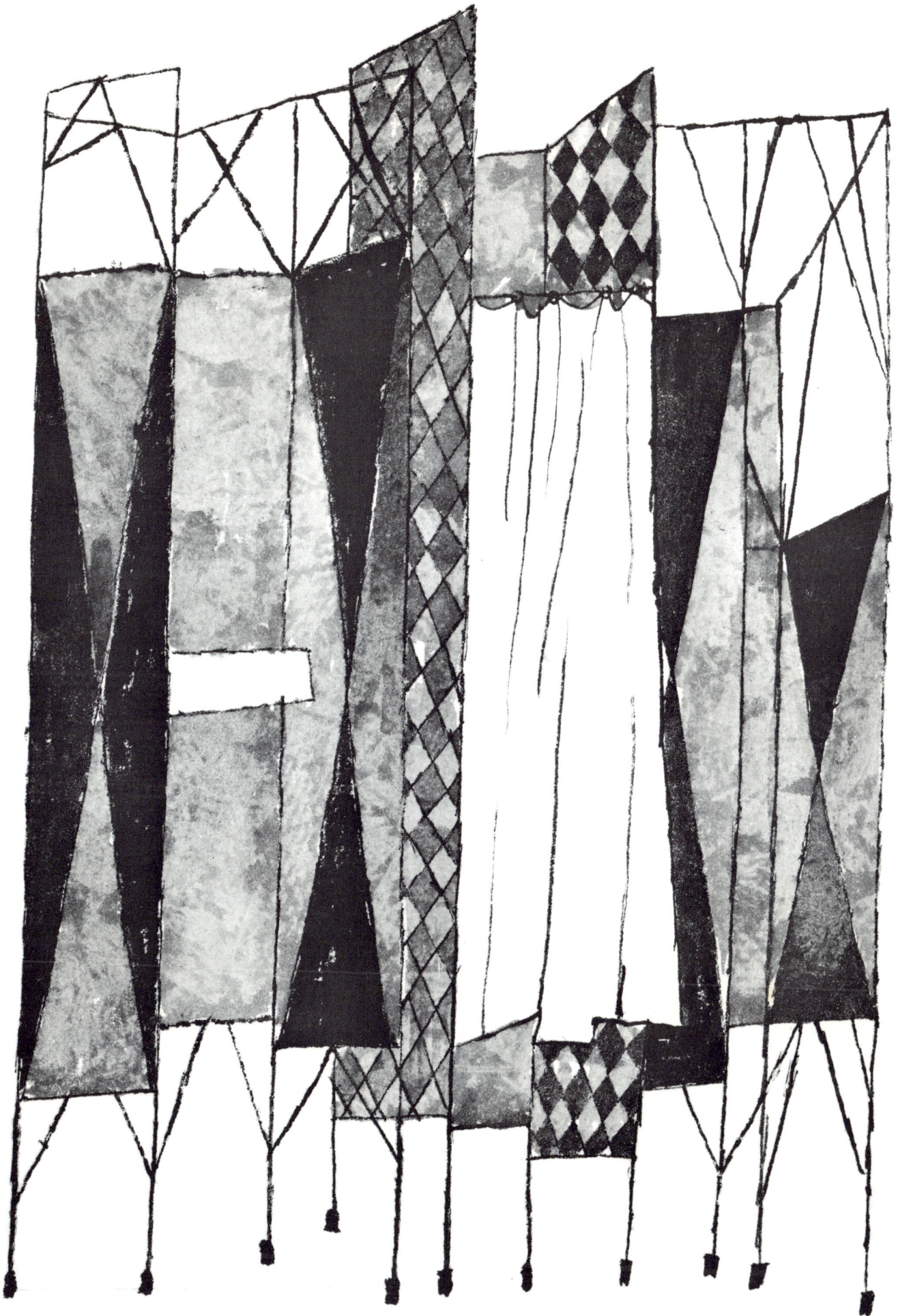

From the moment at which a painter begins to strike figures of color upon a surface he must become acutely sensitive to the feel, the textures, the light, the relationships which arise before him. At one point he will mold the material ~~according~~ according to an intention. At another he may yield intention — perhaps his whole concept, to emerging forms, to new implications within the painted surface. Idea itself — ideas, many ideas move back and forth across his mind as a constant traffic dominated perhaps by larger currents and directions, by what he wants to think. Thus idea rises to the surface, grows, changes as a painting grows and develops. So one must say that painting is both creative and responsive. It is an intimately communicative affair between the painter and his painting, a conversation back and forth, the painting telling the painter even as it receives its shape and form.

Here too, the inward critic is ever at hand, perpetually advising and casting doubt. Here the work is overstated; there it is thin; in another place, a warning that muddiness

is threatening; somewhere else it has lost ~~connection its~~
connection with the whole; here it looks
like an exercise in paint alone; there preserve
an area. Thus the critic, sometimes staying
the hand of the painter, sometimes demanding
a fresh approach, sometimes demanding
that a whole work be abandoned— and
sometimes not succeeding, for the will
may be stubborn enough to ~~so~~ override
such good advice.

I have spoken of the tug of war
between idea and image which at an earlier
time in my painting had plagued me so
greatly. I could not reconcile that conflict by simply abandoning idea, as
so many artists were doing. Such an
approach may indeed simplify painting,
but it also removes it from the arena of
challenging, adult, fully intellectual and
mature practice. For me, there would be little
reason for painting if idea were not to emerge
from the work. I cannot look upon myself or upon
man generally as a merely behaving species. If there
is value it rests upon the human ability to have
idea, and indeed upon the stature of the idea itself.

The painting of the Red Beast "Allegory",
is an idea painting. It is also a highly emotional painting, and I hope that it is still
primarily an image, a paint image. I began
the painting, as I have said, with no established
idea, only with the sense of a debt to be
paid and with a clamoring of images,
many of them. But as to the fire itself,
and as to fires, I had many ideas, a whole

sub-continent of ideas, none of which would be executed to measure, but anyone of which might rise to become the dominating force in the painting. So it was with a series of paintings which I made during and after the time of the fire animal. There was the painting "Brothers". Paint, yes, but also reunion, reconciliation, end of war, pain of strong feeling, family, brothers. There was the painting called "City of Dreadful Night," a forest of television aerials, lines in paint splashes of light, or heads of ancient demons tangled in the antennae - a sombre building with moldering Greek heads. All of these images arose out of paint, yes, but they also arose out of the somewhat ominous implications of television for the mind, for the culture. Out of a chain of connective ideas, responding to paint and color, rises the image, the painted idea. Thus the work may turn in an amusing direction, in a satirical direction. Or sometimes I find images - image ideas which are capable of great implication, which can be built up to a high point of expressive power, at least for my purposes.

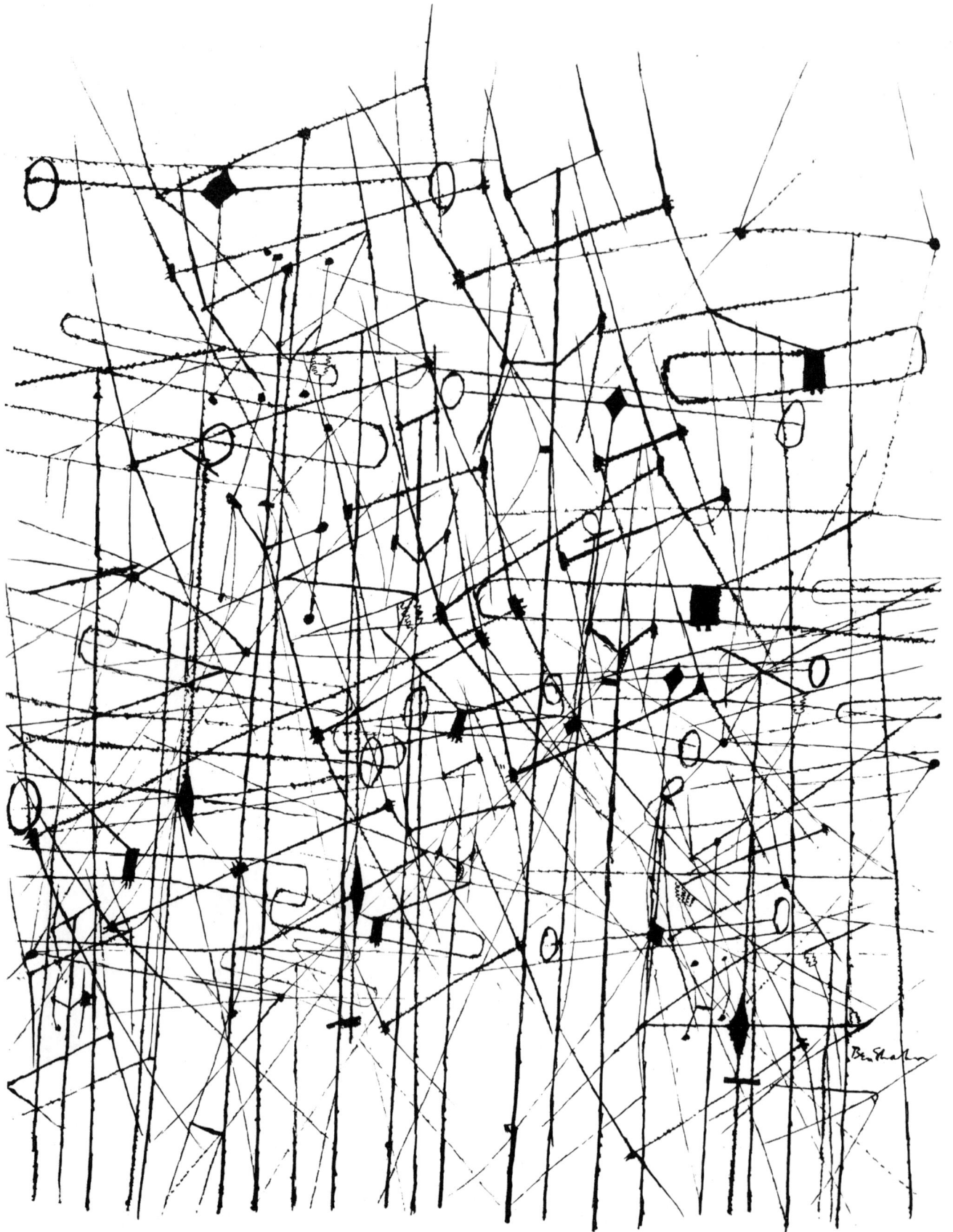

I cannot question that such a two-way communication has always constituted the painting process, sometimes with greater insistence of idea, sometimes with less—or none. Personal style, be it that of Michelangelo, or that of Tintoretto, or of Titian or of Giotto has always been that personal rapport which has developed between an artist and his medium.

So I feel that painting is by no means a limited medium, neither limited to idea alone, nor to paint alone. I feel that painting is able to contain ~~important~~ whatever one thinks and all that he is. The images which may be drawn out of colored materials may have depth and luminosity measured by the artist's own power to recognize and respond to such qualities, and to develop them. Painting may reflect, even brilliantly, the very limitations of an artist, the innocence of a Rousseau, of a Bombois, of a John Kane. Painting can contain and it has at various times contained the whole of scholarship. Painting can contain the politician in a Daumier, the insurgent in a Goya, the suppliant in a Macaccio. It is not a spoken idea alone, nor a legend, nor a simple use nor intention which forms which forms what I have called the biography of a painting. It is rather the wholeness of thinking and feeling within an individual; it is partly his time and place; it his partly his childhood or even his adult fears and pleasures, and it is very greatly thinking what he wants to think.

"For the sake of a few lines," wrote Rilke," one must see many cities, men and things. One must know the animals, one must feel how the birds fly and know the gesture with which small flowers open in the morning. One must be able to think back to roads in unknown regions, to unexpected meetings and to partings which one had long seen coming; to days of childhood that are still unexplained, to parents that one had to hurt when they brought one some joy and one did not grasp it (it was a joy for someone else); to childhood illness that so strangely began with a number of profound and grave transformations, to days in rooms withdrawn and quiet and to mornings by the sea, to the sea itself, to seas, to nights of travel that rushed along on high and flew with all the stars — and it not yet enough if one may think all of this. One must have memories of many nights of love, none of which was like the others, of the screams of woman in labor, and of light, white, sleeping woman in childbed, closing again. But one must also have been beside the dying, one must have sat beside the dead in the room with the open window and the fitful noises. And still it is not enough to have memories. One must be able to forget them when they are many, and one must have the great patience to wait until they come again. For it is not yet the memories themselves. Not until they have turned to blood within us, to glance, to gesture, nameless and no longer to be distinguished from ourselves—not until then can it happen that in a most rare hour the first word of a verse arises in their midst and goes forth from them"

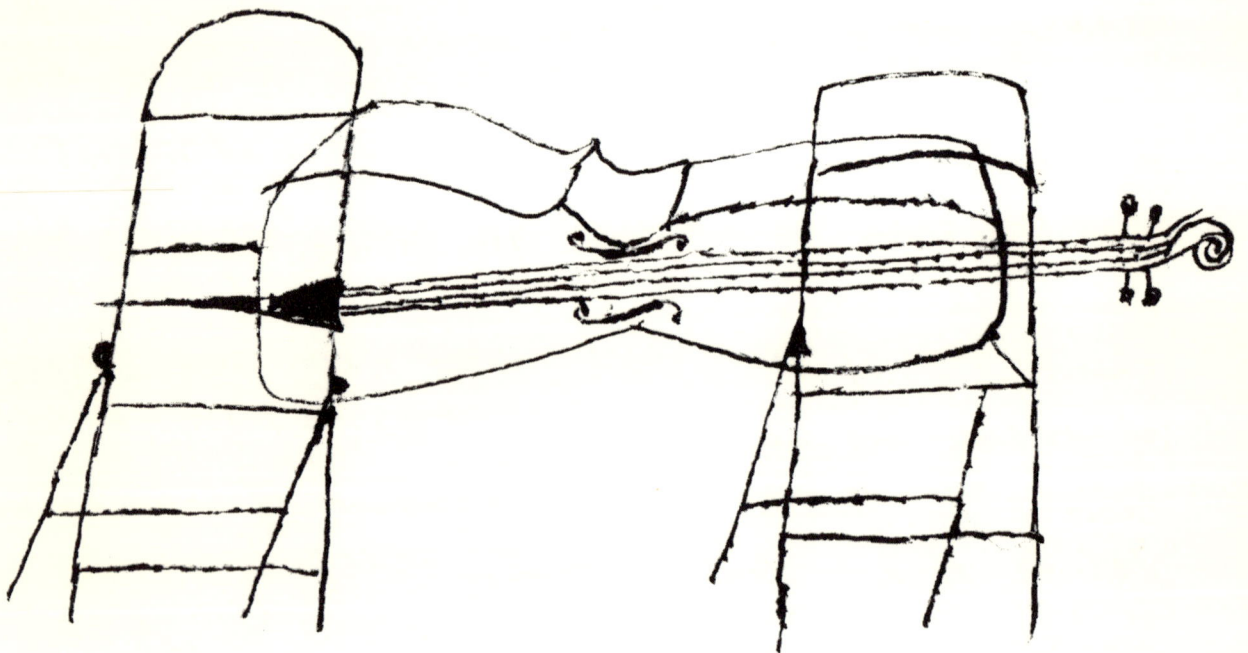

NOTES.

The line drawings and prints in this book are in the artist's collection. Other plates are listed below in page order.

Allegory (*frontispiece*). Collection Bill Bomar.

Blind Botanist.

The Defaced Portrait. Collection Mr. and Mrs. Hoke Levin.

Walker Evans. Collection Walker Evans.

Nicholas C. Collection Lester Avnet.

Kuboyama (*"Lucky Dragon" series*). Collection Robert Straus.

Prometheus. Collection Philadelphia Museum of Art.

Incubus. Collection Mr. and Mrs. Emmons R. Bahan.

Four Piece Orchestra. Collection Mr. and Mrs. S. J. Perelman.

Italian Landscape I. Collection Walker Art Center, Minneapolis, Minnesota.

Labyrinth. Collection Mr. and Mrs. George W. W. Brewster.

This is Nazi Brutality. Collection The Museum of Modern Art, New York.

Liberation. Collection James Thrall Soby.

Goyescas. Collection Paul Roebling.

The Red Stairway. Collection City Art Museum of St. Louis.

Italian Landscape II. Collection Mr. and Mrs. Irving Levick.

Reconstruction. Collection Whitney Museum of American Art, New York.

Cherubs and Children. Collection Whitney Museum of American Art.

Second Allegory. Collection Krannert Art Museum, University of Illinois, Urbana, Illinois.

East 12th Street. Collection Mr. and Mrs. Albert Hackett.

Byzantine Isometric. Collection Mr. and Mrs. Stanley Wolf.

Acknowledgment is made to the following for their cooperation in obtaining photographs of a number of the illustrations in this book: The Museum of Modern Art, New York; Walker Art Center, Minneapolis; Whitney Museum of American Art, New York; Downtown Gallery, New York.

Ben Shahn